The Greatest Treasure

An anthology of verse composed
even as the shadows fall.

Marius Oelschig

Marius Oelschig

The Greatest Treasure

ISBN 978-0-9948479-4-2

Printed and bound in the USA by CreateSpace, an Amazon company.

Cover design by Dan Huckle, Okotoks, AB, Canada
- danhuckle.com -
based upon the inspiration of Zasha and Zayden Oelschig Rabie.
Author photo courtesy of the Western Wheel, Okotoks, AB

First printing March 2018

Marius Oelschig

Dedication

My simple haiku says it all:

If water is life ...
How difficult to describe
My love for my wife.

Marius Oelschig

The Greatest Treasure

The title of one of the books I wrote for my grandchildren is *Jak of the Bushveld*. Two chapters deal with a treasure hunt on a farm in the northern Bushveld of South Africa, up on the Limpopo River, during the winter school vacation. A grandfather places "clues", in the form of simple riddles and rhymes, in small bottles all around the farm ... each clue leading to the next. His grandchildren and some friends solve each riddle and eventually find the "treasure", of course, which turns out to be original Bushman paintings on the walls of a cave on the farm. Upon finding the treasure, the children also find the final rhyme, which reads:

> *No matter what your fortune be*
> *Your greatest gift is what you see.*
> *Of all the jewels we may find,*
> *The greatest treasure is in the mind.*

... hence the title of this anthology.

The poetry in this collection reflects my thoughts and feelings across several decades. I'm hoping that all readers will find something to please them. Some of this was written for my grandchildren and I trust that you will forgive the silly little poems and rhymes ... which brought me, and I hope them too, so much pleasure. Perhaps they'll read them to their own children one day.

Having been a career soldier, there is also war poetry in this anthology. My dearest wish for my grandchildren is that they are spared the dreadful experience of armed conflict. My own experience of human nature would suggest otherwise, but we live in hope.

What cannot be avoided, however, is the passage of years. It happens to us all. Perhaps, when the time comes for them, those that remain will find some solace in these pages for I will not be with them, to hold their hand, when the shadows fall. This is my gift to you all.

Okotoks, AB
Canada
March 2018

The Greatest Treasure

Part One

... with the sound of the guns ever in the
background.

Our God and soldier we alike adore,
When at the brink of ruin, not before;
After deliverance both alike requited,
Our God forgotten and our soldiers slighted.

Francis Quarles
1592-1644

1

Marius Oelschig

The Boy

He was only a boy
When he went to war,
Called to fight the Nation's foes.
He showed no fear,
But had a knot in his gut
That only a soldier knows.

Hunger and thirst
Were everyday wares
And soldiers his only kin.
His hands were hard
And his body was strong
'Tho his heart was quaking within.

It's the mothers that hear
Their sons at prayer,
As the Shadow of Death draws nigh,
Who'd rid the Earth
Of this dreadful curse
That calls their boys to die.

The boy returned
To his mother's embrace
And wept as she held him tight.
But those wretched tears
Were not for his fears,
They were for boys that were lost in the fight.

December 1980

New-found Friends

They learned to fight, the new-found friends;
Taught to handle the tools of war.
Then they journeyed forth to ply their skills
As soldiers on foreign shores.

They learned to laugh, the new-found friends;
Boys in the land of men,
As, beyond their ken, their fate was sealed
With a sigh, and the stroke of a pen.

They went to war, the new-found friends,
And they entered the Gates of Hell.
Angels seemed to keep them safe
As others around them fell.

The mayhem and slaughter raged on and on.
It never seemed to end.
The laughter died, replaced by tears
At the grave of every new-found friend.

1978

A Soldier's Gifts

On his farm he often lay
On his back on the hard-packed dirt
As the sweat of his toil
Slowly turned to mud
On the back
Of his threadbare shirt.

The soldier lay
On his back again
And the memories rushed in a flood
As he watched the clouds scud overhead
And the blood from his wounds
Turned to mud.

The tears that rolled
Across his cheeks
Turned to mud as they fell to the earth.
His sweat, his blood
And his final tears -
Gifts to the land of his birth.

May 1980

The Missing Missed

He went to War. He did not return.
How do you *think* I feel?
What a terrible question to ask, my friend
With my heart encased in steel.

No one came from "the Army";
They sent me a letter instead.
It came in the autumn as I recall.
He's "missing in action" it said.

Did he think of me as he perished,
Or does he think of me now?
Is he wounded and helpless in hospital?
When can I see him, and how?

Did he remember his home on the veld
During some terrible fight?
Was he killed in the glory of morning?
Did he die at the dead of night?

I look at his clothes in the cupboard.
Do I cast them out ... or not?
And his motorcycle out there in the shed,
Do we leave it there to rot?

A candle will be in the window
Until the day that I know.
Maybe they'll find him in some lonely place
Where only a soldier would go.

It's been five years to the day.
I've got to accept that he's gone,
But I'll never, ever surrender my love ...
O, when will my boy come home?

July 1987

Known but to God

There was a light in his eyes as the soldier died,
A light that nobody would see.
T 'was a glint of pride in the knowledge he'd died
For his calling — defending the free.

Despite what he saw of the horrors of War,
He was ready to do what was right.
So, together he stood with others that would;
Warriors, willing to fight.

With his terrible skill to maim and to kill,
There were few that respected his role.
Yet, without any thought for the freedom he brought,
There were many that damned his soul.

Though he spent all his time in the dirt and the grime,
With the Angel of Death above,
There was always a part of his hardened heart
That yearned for peace and love.

He was found at last after days had passed
But nobody knew who he was.
He was buried that day in the field where he lay
At the foot of a soldier's cross.

Nobody to weep when the Endless Sleep
Drew a veil o'er his pain and strife.
May the soft, gentle rains o'er the hills and the plains
Be the tears for this soldier's life.

April 2017

The White Flower

War engulfs the land
In flaming rage,
And nature feels the scourge
Of some demented soul.
Creation's plan, writ large
Upon this ancient page,
Is scorched and scarred;
Remittance of life's demonic toll?

Marauding tracks crush
Unsuspecting life
As roaring, raiding monsters
Carve their trail
Across a landscape,
Innocent of strife.
This placid place, now witness
To destruction and travail.

Once-noble structures smashed.
Their smouldering beams
Leave wretched, ragged ruins;
Sad memories in their stead.
Yet in the wake of death
And shattered dreams
A small white flower, triumphant,
Lifts its head.

July 1981

A Song of Hope

Dusk settles
On a soldier's life,
On hard days of a hardened man.
Failing eyes that saw the worst
That man can wreak, gaze westwards
Where sunset veils dreadful peaks
No less severe for gentler hues.

Was his a life well-led?
Or will barbarians rule our world?
Will children ever have the right
To choose the way they live?
To love, to laugh, to sing?
To take whatever
Wending way they may?

Then, a child he loves
Lifts up her voice in song,
Touching hearts,
Imploring that she yet be heard.
Thus, hope and joy still have their place
In this mad world grown numb with grief and pain.
The fight was *not* in vain.

January 2014

Sonnet of the Guardians

Why is the human race so prone to strife?
Why can we not exist in harmony?
Instead, we ever reach for sword and knife;
When will we learn to let our quarrels be?
Creation's millstone has a human face;
Fanatics who are driven by their creed,
Who, flouting opposition and disgrace,
Would subjugate the world to fuel their greed.
But, there are some who will not bend the knee,
Whose loyalty and courage you may trust;
Who cannot bear the thought of slavery
And who will pay whatever price we must.
When threats emerge, we do not turn and flee.
The Guardians of this sacred land are we!

February 2015

Note. This sonnet was drafted in 1960 during my final year of high school at Grey College in Bloemfontein, South Africa. I completed it in 2015. It is being published in 2018 … thanks to the unflagging efforts of my esteemed English teacher, Mr Jannie Earp, who somehow managed to plant the seed of literature in the breast of an adventurous, sport-loving teenager. As Mr. Jaap Rousseau, our renowned Afrikaans teacher, would say, "Aanhouer wen!"

Marius Oelschig

Fading Away

Can I live now as fiercely once I did?
Or need I tame the demons lurking near?
Has time taught me to better leave unsaid
Opinions I was once inclined to share?
Perhaps the barbs that wounded, long to heal,
Will chasten me and damp the ardent flame.
Cautious now my judgement to reveal
With less regard for instinct than for shame.
For, having led the stirring warrior's life,
More splendid than I'd readily admit,
Perhaps the time has come to douse the fire
And to a less ferocious life submit.
But, how to live with passions that endure?
The balm of time has ever been the cure.

November 2011

Row upon Row

Row upon row of
White crosses
And headstones,
Marking mankind's wars.
Symbols
Of human sacrifice,
Scars
Of humanity's flaws.

December 2017

Marius Oelschig

Part Two

Grandchildren are God's gift to you ...
for not having killed your own children.

Anonymous

Marius Oelschig

My Own Little Sarie Marais

I remember the song that I sang for so long,
A song about Sarie Marais.
It's a tale so old of a soldier bold
Who pines for a damsel fair.
Well, Sarie Marais could never compare
With my little brown-eyed dove.
And every time I see a green thorn tree
I dream of the girl that I love.

The mielie land with the red-brown sand
Is sadly not the place I can go
To see the curly hair and the face so fair
Of the prettiest girl I know.
So, my days I'll bide by the riverside
As I wait for the time to arrive
To be close to the one who's my moon and sun,
Whose bright smile keeps me alive.

She's the sweetest thing that makes my heart sing
But, like Sarie Marie of the song,
Though she's so dear to me she's way across the sea
And we've been apart for too long.
Now the soldier so old who once was so bold
Builds castles in the Bushveld air,
As he waits for the day when he'll fly away
To join his own little Sarie Marais.

March 2004

This Special Day

Zasha was born on Christmas Day
A gift from Heaven above.
She was sent to Earth, this bundle of joy,
To spread happiness, laughter and love.

She came to us in Edmonton;
How the time flies away.
Our brown-eyed, curly-haired little girl
Is five years old today.

I pray that you read this little poem
Each and every year.
And when you do, remember your Grumps
With a smile and not a tear.

Happy Birthday, Kiewiet and Merry Christmas!

December 2006

Marius Oelschig

Springtime

The springtime has come and the heat of the sun
Will drive all the cold away.
Boys and girls with their caps and curls
Will go out in the sunshine to play.

They laugh as they ride on the swing and the slide,
As they play with Scruffy the dog.
They forgot about sleet and cold little feet,
They forget about ice, snow and fog.

Tiny plants sprout and the flowers come out
It's a wonderful sight to see.
I tell you, my dear, it's a great time of year.
It's springtime, the best time for me.

October 2005

The Bushveld Bunch

Whenever you're lonely with nothing to do,
Just call on the Bushveld Bunch.
They'll keep you amused with a story or two,
The wonderful Bushveld Bunch.
There's Tuffy the tortoise, a lion called Ruff,
A squirrel called Squirt, and if that's not enough
There's Jacko the monkey and a bird that you'll
like;
A little blue owl called Ike.

It's tough not to love them, they like to have fun,
The boys of the Bushveld Bunch.
They live in the Land of the African sun;
The wonderful Bushveld Bunch.
They live in the bush; they don't like the town,
Their very best friend is Tickey the Clown.
If you'd like to meet them just get up and go,
They're waiting to say, "Hello!"

Marius Oelschig

Who am I?

I've got feathers like a bird,
But I can't fly
'Cos I'm too big to stay in the sky.
My legs are long, but that's not all
I lay an egg the size of a ball.
Who am I?

The Cool Turkey

There was a cool turkey named Guy
With a burning ambition to fly.
He flew high and low ...
Where the jet aircraft go,
And now he's cold turkey on rye.

Watching Zayden Grow

Zayden is a happy chap,
Especially when he's had his nap.
He laughs and plays and tries to talk
And very soon he's going to walk.
Then you'll have to know your stuff
'Cos little boys are really tough.
So, Zasha, some advice for you
To help with what you're going through:
Play with cars and other toys
That seem to interest little boys.
Treat little boys like little Kings ...
And they'll stay away from all **your** things.

May 2005

Mrs Barrow

Growing up is really tough
But I'm learning every day.
So it's nice to have a special friend
To help me on my way.

My first school years were really great,
But I know that this is true;
I'll thank my lucky stars one day
For a wonderful teacher like you.

Zasha Oelschig Rabie
(With a little help from her
Grumpi in the Bushveld)

July 2008

Remember Him

Santa Claus was here last night,
Passing with the speed of light.
Now little girls and little boys
Are playing with their Christmas toys.

But let's remember, if we can
How this special day began.
Well, long ago in crib so small
Christ was born to save us all.

As Silent Night we softly sing,
How should we remember Him?
With peace on Earth and lots of joy
For *every* little girl and boy.

Christmas 2008

Goodbye Winter

Warm sunshine is back;
No frozen toes and noses.
Snowmen wave goodbye.

April 2013

The Explorer

He's four years old, with big brown eyes.
He has a great big heart for a boy his size.
He's just been visiting his African friends,
Down at the tip where the Continent ends.

He crashed off a slide and got burnt by the sun,
But he thinks that's all just part of the fun.
Now that he's gone we miss him so much,
But he made us promise to keep in touch.

He called today to say Happy New Year,
But he also made his Grumpi swear
To send a message every week or two
So he can keep up to date with the Bushveld
crew.

1 January 2009

The Hadedas

Harry and Harriette,
Our Hadeda friends,
Enjoy the sunset
As another day ends.
They're taking a rest
From all of the walking,
From all of the flying
And all of the squawking.

They're nosy and noisy
And, for what it's worth,
They must be the ugliest
Birds on Earth.
But we have to accept
That they're here to stay
Like the sunset at the end
Of a perfect day.

December 2011

Marius Oelschig

Your Roots Are in the Veld

You may be Canadian-born, my child,
For that's what the record shows,
But your roots are in the veld my dear,
Where the *suikerbossie* grows.

Your home is in the ice and snow
With the Rockies at your door,
But it's that scent of the veld after the rain
That will lure you back to this shore.

The blood of your kin is in the soil,
For this Land has taken its toll.
Their spirits roam o'er these sunny plains
Where the sunsets soothed their soul.

The Greatest Treasure

You will return to the veld, my child,
You'll be drawn by the sound of the drum.
You'll remember the call of the *Piet-my-Vrou*
And like a moth to the flame, you will come.

Your roots are in the veld, my dear.
Soon you'll hear the call of the drum.
You'll be back to see your kin return
To the veld, when the time has come.

November 2009

Marius Oelschig

Part Three

Reflections in haiku

A poem is the very image of
life expressed in its eternal truth.
                    Shelley (1821)

Marius Oelschig

Haiku

For those not in the know, haiku is a traditional form of Japanese poetry. Each poem consists of only three lines. The first line is composed of exactly five syllables, the second of seven and the third again of only five, for a total of seventeen syllables. Rhyming plays no significant part, whereas the natural world is the almost overwhelming subject of haiku. In keeping with the minimalist style, many haiku poems are untitled.

> *An old silent pond ...*
> *A frog jumps into the pond,*
> *Splash! Silence again.*

This haiku poem was composed by Basho Matsuo (1644 – 1694), considered to be the greatest haiku poet of all time.

My own modest attempts at haiku follow.

Marius Oelschig

The Greatest Treasure

Laughter of children –
Tiny drops of purest joy;
The essence of life.

Snowflakes gently fall,
Leaving a soft, cold blanket
On our molten Earth.

Marius Oelschig

All creatures alike
Waiting for the light of dawn
To live another day.

Softly falls the rain
Bringing life to everything
Existing on this orb.

Would there ever be wars
On this small, fragile planet
If Nature could choose?

Prowling, hungry trout
Ascend from the murky depths
To feed on small flies.

Senseless, arrogant fools
Defile our beautiful world
Just because they can.

The poor work the soil
To produce the many goods
For kings to endure.

Clouds of land-bound gulls

Swooping and shrieking for joy

In their gift of flight.

A tiny ant falls

Onto a mirror-like lake –

Fodder for the fish.

Spiders Fly

A slim silken thread -

Allowing spiders to fly

All around the world.

Wilderness

Is my print the first

To fall upon this one spot

Of our vast planet?

The Greatest Treasure

Marius Oelschig

Part Four

Growing old gratefully, even as the shadows fall.

Old age is charming,
but what a misfortune
that it lasts so short a time.

Emile Augier
1880

Marius Oelschig

Running from the Reaper

With tireless tread he roves across the land,
A sharpened scythe forever in his hand.
Though watchful eyes peruse his every stride
We mortals know - we have no place to hide.

For those of us who fear this deadly jerk,
Who goes about his grim and gruesome work,
There is a way to duck his nasty knife,
To add a few more years to every life.

The first thing you must do is ... have a beer.
It gives you time to think and calms your fear.
Then, using all your guile and crafty wit,
Draw up your plan to dodge the smelly ... twit.

"Keep moving", is my best advice to you.
"One step ahead", is really what to do.
Don't ever stop, don't ever quit the game.
He'll get you while you rest your weary frame.

Stand up to him should he approach too near,
Look in his eyes and show you have no fear.
Then scare him off by doing something frightening
Like parachuting, downhill skiing, mountain
biking.

He'll get you in the end; you know that's fate.
So, don't sit there like some flabby piece of bait.
Make it tough for him; go out and have some fun
And enjoy those extra years you will have won.

My span is growing short upon this coil,
But my life has not been *only* sweat and toil.
I've burned my candle right down to the nub
And if the Reaper *really* wants me ...

                    he can find me in the pub.

September 2016

Pounds, Shillings and Pence

It has taken me fully three-score-years-and-fifteen ,
Well beyond my biblical span of "... and-ten" you
will note,
To finally, but sadly comprehend that there are but
Three distinct and separate strata of creatures
That populate this Earth:
The Strong, the Weak
And those whose very existence is predicated upon
Their preying on the Weak ...
The Dastardly.

Aye, it took some time for the denarii to drop
But, unlike the impecunious modern penny,
Surely this delayed epiphany yet retains,
If only in my own intellectual estimation,
Some small measure of value.
For, were this insight to serve as basis for
consideration of
Ancient norms, practices, conventions, even laws,
Yet might it guide modern youth to better
understand their world.

Spartans, as we know, eliminated the frail and the
weak.
Deformed babies, the crippled aged and other
societal burdens
Were abandoned, exposed to the elements and left
to die.
Were Spartans Strong or were they Dastardly?
I'd wager that modern politically-correct
adolescents
Would plumb for the latter.
Let them explain, in practical terms, how they aim
to manage
A world populated by more than ten billion souls.

Spartans held that children were the property of
the State.
Is that not what the modern State espouses?
While condemning the notion of the survival of the
fittest,
Modern leaders defend the rights of children to the
extent
That parents' rights are so severely restricted and
circumscribed that
Children are effectively wards of the State.
Yet the tenet of "we know best what is best for
you"

The Greatest Treasure

Is neither judicious, productive nor beneficial ... but
Dastardly.

Flogging for spitting. Summarily hanging horse-
thieves.
Prison for stealing. Transportation of the unfit.
Were our ancestors Strong or Dastardly?
Certainly not Weak!
What would *they* make of modern norms?
Would they accept - or reject - our polluted world,
Our sundered society, our sullied statesmen?

We strive, we assert, for Justice;
The Gilded Cup our cherished goal.
Yet we reject, in our humanity, the primitive
But righteous eye for eye and tooth for tooth.
Should we not shamefully concede that we now
Offer more protection, more care, more comfort
To the sinners than to the sinned against,
Uplifting the Dastardly; failing the Weak?

So, as we splutter and choke on our journey
Midst the noxious fumes of progress,
Who amongst us does not yearn for the serene,
Bucolic existence of yesteryear, when Roman roads
Were trod by bullock's hooves, wooden wheels and
soldier's shoes?
To hell with modernity! ... your psyche shrieks,

Marius Oelschig

You'd much prefer the old Romanus epoch of
Librae, solidi and denarii - pounds, shillings and
that damned penny.
You think?

18 January 2018

To be Equal

I'm led to believe,
By philosophers, no less,
That every human life,
One's biblical three-score years
And ten, I guess,
Can be neatly undone,
Detached and divided,
Packaged and wrapped,
And readily stuffed
Into six distinctive drawers –
Compartments, if you like:
Birth and growth;
Emotionality (is that a word?);
Aspiration;
Conflict (of course); and
Mortality.
If that is not equality
In its purest form –
Then nothing is.

June 2015

Bad Poetry?

There are those who will disagree but,
according to me, there is no bad poetry.
There are no bad poets – some are simply
better than others;
Far better, perhaps, or just with greater skill.
We can't all be Babe Ruth,
Or Tiger Woods, or Garth Brooks, or
Shakespeare for that matter, but we can
As best we can, express our thoughts and
feelings, articulate, through poetry,
In the common words we say, the passion and
the pain that drives our everyday.
Like playing baseball with friends, or playing a
round of golf,

Or singing a favourite song, or losing a job, or
being dumped by the only girl
That you have ever truly loved, or spilling hot
coffee all over your
New pants at the first sight of ... the new girl in
your life, who
Doesn't even know who you are.
Can that ever be bad?
If a man, who is not a carpenter, is asked to
build a bench, perhaps
Decides for himself to build a bench, and if he
should make something
That looks like a bench, feels and smells and is
used like a bench,
Is it not a bench? Is he not a carpenter?
It may not be the finest bench
In the village or town.
You may not want it or like it, but it is a bench.
And if a man, who is a poet, decides to write
bad poetry,
With the purpose, intentionally, of writing
really bad poetry; to scoff,
To deride or to goad. Were he to succeed,
would you agree that he
Has written good poetry?

And if a man, not a poet, is moved to write a
poem to tell the world
That he has fallen in love, and someone –
having never read poetry –
Is moved to tears, remembering that he, or she,
was also once in love,
Can it ever be a bad poem?
Everyone has a story to tell; a unique,
wonderful story that
Only *they* can tell. There is no shame in being
unschooled,
In fumbling with the tools.
One can always learn. Are we ever too old to
learn?
For it is the *story* that people wish to hear; of
everyday life,
In words that they know, recognise,
comprehend; that bring them joy,
Which they may repeat when their own scabby
life beats them into retreat
From the joy they once knew.
And if the teller were to choose poetry
As the method of telling, can that be wrong?
Does that make the poetry bad?

The Greatest Treasure

What would be sad would be the failure to tell
the story, to hear the story,
Whether in elegantly crafted, flowing, magical
poetry, prose or rhyming verse
That will cause even the snotty poetry snob to
pause – to listen to the story.
And when the story is written or told, the poet
– good poet, bad poet –
Will feel and grasp that same liberating,
Addictive, exquisite joy of
Creation ... of poetry.

April 2016

Debate Me

Don't hate me, debate me.
I stole your land, you say.
Was it ever yours?
Don't hate me today for what
Your ancestors did yesterday;
Trading what they had
For what they could get.
Don't hate me, hate them.

The sins of the father, like shadows,
Fall upon his sons
And his daughters.
Don't pin your father's sins on me.
You want to be my equal?
So be!
You believe that you're better than me?
Prove it!

The Greatest Treasure

You said that you'd
Do things better than me.
You've had your chance and ...
You didn't.
You blamed me for the mess
You claimed your people were in.
You've done your best, you say, but now
Your people flee from the mess they're in.

The entire world gave you every chance
And the benefit of the doubt.
You were given all the advice,
And the treasure, that you needed ...
But you blew it.
Be that as it may ... but now accept
That we're in this together.
Debate me, don't hate me.

January 2018

The Writers Group

Write Away!, as you may have heard,
Is a group that fixates on ... "the word".
So I scribble and scratch
At products that match
My skill at producing ... a turd!

As we meet for a couple of drinks,
And despite what my family thinks,
We agree, as a group,
That my work is like poop
For, to put it quite plainly ... it stinks!

June 2013

Miser's Gold

Happiness flows from the Spring of Life
But is lost in the Desert of Years
And the tears of joy that ever we shed
Wash away in the River of Tears.

The joy that we've felt as we've watched you grow
Are the memories that we retain
Like a Miser's Gold. Kept safe in our heart
For the long, lonely years that remain.

The dreams that you have are dreams of our own
And we share every moment of dread
At the hurdles you face and the battles to come
On the hazardous journey ahead.

Now, a summit achieved, and acclaim in the air
We are proud of what you have done.
And we add to our store of Miser's Gold
For the long, cold winter to come.

Live for the moment and amass all the joy
As you watch your future unfold.
But open your heart ... and remember to add
To *your* hoard of Miser's Gold.

February 2014

Four Seasons

I'm sick of Winter's cold embrace,
Of staring at its frigid face.
My thoughts now turn to Spring.
My soul demands its share of heat,
Of worshipping at Summer's feet
Whilst dreading Autumn's sting.

February 2015

Marius Oelschig

The Struggling Poet

A bubbling brew that steams and stews,
Words threatening to spew.
Like lava within,
Lipping the brim.
An explosion wanting a fuse.

Consuming his thoughts, his nights, his days,
Words, lost in a maze
Of creative pain.
His energy drained,
"O, give me relief!" he prays.

Drowning in doubt and flagging desire
The light of Hope must expire.
The Muse resists.
The poet persists.
He will never submit
To be branded unfit —
To be led, by his peers, to his pyre.

July 2015

Puddles

After the rain
There are puddles everywhere.
Large or small,
Muddy or clear,
They are all filled with the same
Life-sustaining gift.

After the rain
All puddles reflect
The glory of the sky
And the stars
Or the sparkle
Of a sunny day.

After the rain
We must make time
To delight
In the magic
That the puddles reflect –
Before they disappear.

June 2015

The Medieval Castle of Terena

I stand beneath the soaring walls of
The Castle of Terena, looking up,
Past the ramparts to the ponderous, dark
Winter-clouds that would have been there
As those early masons, bones aching,
Backs breaking, wrestled with slimy-wet rocks,
Savaging their bare knuckles on begrudging
granite,
Scrambling to get the day's allotted task done
Just to avoid the monumental wrath
Of the meticulous Master-Mason. Bastard!

I gaze at the rock-blotches on the towering walls,
Each patch telling its own story of
A bullock-cartload and of the Portuguese men,
Maybe women too, that lifted and carried
And hefted and hauled those rocks
To the site, to be manoeuvred and moulded
With the earth's mud and the craftsman's blood
Into strong, stout walls that have stood,
Unbroken, for more than three hundred years.
Did those masons believe that their walls
would last that long?

My soldier's mind catapults me back to ancient
times,
To stand his beat with a sentry, a peasant boy,
On these ageless walls, with familiar shield and
sword,
Trusty old friends, to hand. We allow our eyes to
glide
Over darkening plains as gloom descends
Like a heavy, comforting cowl – cloaking our fear.
Then off, relieved, to the smoky, mellow haze of his
family home
And a bubbling pot of spicy *caldeirada de cabrito*.
Safe and warm, within the walls, the village rests.
The folk then rise once more to daily life; to draw
the water,
Feed the stock and farm the land – and build the
walls.

Yet, crouched in the menacing shadow of Spain,
the peril,
The danger to this Castle and its people remained –
unchanged.
Mounted Castilian knights and their leather-clad
marching men,
Perhaps hordes of galloping, mad-eyed Moors, all
Marauding with lust and loot – and power – their
intent;

Ravaging, savaging the villages and towns that
straddled their path.
The test would come, of walls and men,
When the tide of War crashed upon the Castle of
Terena.
Did those proud, patient masons of yore expect
their walls
To remain standing against the wrath of Time and
Man,
As they did ... as they have ... as they can?

April 2017

Reminder

The alarm on my smart phone,
Keeping me connected.
Reminding me today of a special event;
Maretha King's birthday.
Happy birthday, Mariet!
My memories of you, sharp;
Sharp as the Angolan sun
On soft, white beaches;
Soft as a tropical breeze
On sun-scorched skin;
Cool as the local Cuca beer
On parched, salty lips.

Ah, those lazy days
When we lived for the break
At the end of the week.
Living like kings (ha-ha)
In that tropical paradise.
Energy to burn as we surfed,
Sailed and frolicked in the sun.
Indestructible, we were;
The idyll would last forever.
Alas, not to be.
The Terrible **C**
Claimed Mariet.
Already three years ago?

July 2015

Watching Shadows Lengthen

While watching the shadows lengthen and fade
We question the purpose of living.
Can we take pride in the effort we made
And were we, as warriors, forgiving?
Will we be forgotten the moment we pass
Or remembered for long years to come?
Will comrades assembled lift up a glass
In remembrance of battles we won?

These are the questions a soldier must face
When mustered for sunset parade,
When the roll is called at the end of the race
And we're judged for the choices we made.
When the time comes there is One who commands,
With no friends to stand by your side,
And that One is God, meeting Heaven's demands,
Will he bid you to march off with pride?

November 2016

Love is Lo-tech

Despite mankind's stupefying progress
In science and high-technology,
The modern suitor should
Resign himself to the fact that
He must perforce acquire
An archaic linguistic skill
Allowing him to express
His attraction to and
Emotional feelings for
The object of his longing
In terms that do not equate,
For example,
His devastation at separation
To denial of electronics with
The latest social applications,
Favouring rather
Tender, intimate reflections involving
Perhaps, comparisons of eyes and lips or
Texture of skin
With rosebuds or violets or

The Greatest Treasure

Lily-of-the valley
Whilst judiciously avoiding,
Despite undeniable scientific proof,
Any citation of the wholesomeness and
Nutritional appeal of Russian turnips or
The mouth-watering prospect of
Black beer, pig's trotters and sauerkraut;
For, unless an adequate level of skill
In romantic articulation
Is mastered and suitably applied,
The lovelorn suitor will achieve neither
Yearned-for orgasmic fulfilment nor
The extension of his lineage
Through procreation ...
As poets do!

February 2018

Regret

I've stood in the mighty Rockies
With their mantle of winter's white.
I've seen the clouds of migrant geese
In their majestic flight.
I've felt the touch of a baby,
The embrace of a loving wife.
But,
I've been to war and I've heard the guns
And I've seen men lose their life.

I've heard the lark in the meadow
And the night-jar after dark;
The rumblings of hungry lions
And the jackal's midnight bark.
I've savoured the rain after thirsting;
Sipping heavy dust-laden drops
As the earth revives when the wetness arrives
And the drought fades into the past.

The Greatest Treasure

I've touched the frost on the thistle
When winter sears one's soul,
When nature seems to shudder and shrink
With the coming of the cold.
I've seen the first shy blossoms,
Delicate and bedewed,
Reveal themselves to a wanting world
Rejoicing, with hope renewed.

I've gazed on the works of Masters.
Composers have made me weep;
But, what of the paintings yet to be
And the music still asleep?
So ...
My only regret at the failing years
Is for beauty that will be denied;
For the many wonders I'll never behold
When the darkness deepens at Eventide.

Christmas Eve
2017

Marius Oelschig

Tracks in the Snow

In the soft blown snow
The tracks of many creatures –
Meandering homeward.

February 2018

Marius Oelschig

Explanatory Notes

Canadians, in general, are renowned for being self-effacing and polite. They're probably the only people in the world that apologise to furniture when they bump into it. This is not an apology. These are explanatory notes ... for those that feel they have a bone to pick.

- ✓ The "flaws" on the cover were meant to be. Cool, no?
- ✓ Variable font size in the content? Meant to be! Have a closer look; you may even agree.
- ✓ A bit "skinny" for an anthology? Perhaps, but I wanted something small (and affordable) to give to my friends as gifts.
- ✓ You could write better poetry than me? Great! Send me your next anthology and I'll "crit" it for you ... for free.
- ✓ There are four award-winning poems in this anthology. Which do you consider worthy of such consideration?
- ✓ Real men don't write poetry? Explain that to the Japanese whose Samurai warriors were encouraged to write haiku as part of their training in patience, clarity of thought and discipline.
- ✓ Read *Bad Poetry?* on page 58 (one of the award-winning poems) again.

About the Author

Marius Oelschig is a retired soldier, a former paratrooper, living in the small Town of Okotoks, Alberta ... in the shadow of the Canadian Rockies. He has been writing poetry for his own pleasure for many years. This anthology is his first attempt, at the instigation of his children and grandchildren, at publishing his verse in a *proper* collection of selected poems.

www.ingramcontent.com/pod-product-compliance
Lightning Source LLC
Chambersburg PA
CBHW021934170626
46807CB00007B/3098